"It's Your Responsibility Now!"

The Essentials of Leadership

Delegation

MARK J HOLLINGSWORTH

Copyright © 2013 Mark Hollingsworth

All rights reserved.

ISBN-10:1490424296
ISBN-13:978-1490424293

DEDICATION

To my wife sue for her wonderful support.

CONTENTS

	Acknowledgments	i
1	Introduction	Pg 1
2	"It's Your Responsibility Now!"	Pg 4
3	Symptoms Of Poor Delegation	Pg 11
4	The Fear Of Delegation	Pg 18
5	"What Is It That I Can't Delegate?"	Pg 27
6	Creating Amazing Delegation	Pg 43
7	The Delegation Template	Pg 59
8	Key Learning Points	Pg 67

ACKNOWLEDGEMENTS

I would like to thank CreateSpace and Amazon who have made it possible for new authors to realize their dreams of being published.

1. INTRODUCTION

Welcome to my series of leadership skills books, and to this book on the subject of delegation. The aims and objectives of these books are to provide, through the format of story telling, a guide to acquiring the essential skills needed to be effective in leadership.

These books are based around a character called Quinn Spencer. Quinn has recently been appointed as the divisional manager of 'Geographical Area A' for a company called the Stratum Group Inc. (a fictitious organization). Stratum provides a variety of training solutions across a number of industries. They develop custom-made solutions as well as providing off-the-shelf versions. There are four geographical areas in Stratum, all controlled by the vice-president of sales and marketing Andrew Sachs. Quinn reports directly to Andrew.

Within this book you will see Quinn struggling with a variety of leadership challenges, eventually coming to terms with the power and potential of great delegation. Like all leaders, myself included, delegation involves the emotional challenge of giving up an element of control, and placing trust in other people. All leaders initially find these two elements challenging and somewhat daunting, but those who emerge with the confidence to follow a consistent system of delegation soon find themselves powerfully effective leaders.

Delegation is the skill and discipline of giving someone else a job to do that you can do perfectly well yourself, most likely better than the person you are giving the job to. Delegation is in itself a simple process. However, after 30 years in a variety of leadership positions, I was inspired to write this book as a way of helping myself truly rediscover essential skills of delegation. I personally find it the most challenging part of leadership.

At the end of this book I have summarized the key learning points from each of the chapters in an easy-to-use reference style.

Now let's join Quinn at the beginning of another working week at Stratum Group Inc.

Mark J Hollingsworth
The MJH Leadership Training Centre

2. "IT'S YOUR RESPONSIBILITY NOW!"

Quinn Spencer left home on Monday morning at 7:30 AM to start the second week in an exciting new job at Stratum Group Inc as the new divisional manager. The first week had passed in somewhat of a blur, with a seemingly endless round of meetings and briefings held with the senior leadership team, HR, finance and the division's 35 staff and four direct reports that Quinn was now responsible for. Quinn had been successfully headhunted to this new position, but was still somewhat daunted by the leadership challenges that such a large portfolio and number of staff presented.

Quinn also felt disappointed that very little appeared to have been achieved during the first week; the expressions 'fighting fires' and 'drinking from the fire hose' came too easily to mind!

Stratum Group Inc had its own building, a three-storey construction, in a business park, with a large car park at the front and rear of the building. Quinn parked in the front area and entered the building through the main front doors, saying good morning to the receptionist when passing through the expansive reception area. Quinn's office was in the far left hand corner of the building on the second floor. Sally, Joe and Andrea who managed the other three divisional areas – B, C and D - shared the remainder of the corridor.

Quinn was quickly settled in the office by 8:15 AM, and observed, sadly, how Spartan it still looked. Quinn had not found the time in the first five days last week to even unpack the boxes containing the inevitable personal paraphernalia that one carries around from job to job. Moreover, piles of files, papers, journals to read etc had already begun to fill up the various flat surfaces around the office. Quinn turned on the desktop monitor and opened the email management system and proceeded to quickly handle as many of the emails that could be coped with in the next 35 minutes. Quinn was meeting with the Vice President of Sales and Marketing, Andrew Sachs, at 9 AM and wanted to arrive promptly to continue the good impression Quinn hoped had been established during the first week.

Meeting with Andrew

The VPs office was on the third floor and Quinn reported there at five minutes to nine. The VPs executive assistant Elizabeth invited Quinn to wait at the small conference table in the VPs office. Elizabeth explained, with a smile, that the VP was on "walkabout" but would be back promptly at nine o'clock. Quinn, glad of a few minutes to become more composed, settled into the VPs office at the corner conference table and surveyed the calm, organized environment in which the VP operated.

The walls of the office contained a variety of academic and professional development certificates, two extremely large whiteboards containing what appeared to be a complex series of mind maps. The modest size desk was empty of any paraphernalia, with just an in-tray and out-tray on each corner, a telephone, and a tablet computer sitting in the centre of the desk. To the right of the desk was a separate smaller desk containing the VPs iMac, keyboard and mouse. A desktop credenza containing a small number of manila coloured files was set to the right hand edge. The conference table at Quinn which sitting was an adequate size for six people. The only other chairs in the room were two hard backed ones facing the VPs desk. Quinn wondered how on earth such order was maintained, for Andrew was known to have the largest portfolio and number of staff and to be the busiest VP at Stratum. Promptly at 9 AM Andrew walked into the office and smiled at Quinn and said "Good morning Quinn." Quinn return the compliment.

Andrew walked to his desk, placed a Smartphone he had been carrying onto his desk and picked up the tablet computer. He turned and walked to the conference table and sat down opposite Quinn. Andrew smiled warmly and said, "The agenda that Elizabeth would have sent you last Thursday still stands, unless you wish to add anything to it?" Quinn was somewhat taken aback and struggled to remember even seeing an email last Thursday, let alone an attached agenda. Quinn was still trying to clear emails from Wednesday!

"This should take us no more than 15 minutes," said Andrew briskly, looking down at the agenda now displayed on his tablet. Andrew began to cover a variety of areas that he was delegating responsibility to Quinn for. They included the budget, staffing, decision-making parameters, and working schedules.

Andrew presented the delegated areas in a fluent, logical order, regularly ensuring that Quinn was fully conversant with what was being said and the boundaries being established. As the 15 minutes began to draw to a close Andrew stated that he would always be available for questions and would be checking in with Quinn on Friday to make sure that everything was progressing smoothly.

Quinn was vaguely aware, with the vast amount of information being digested over the past 15 minutes, that at no stage was Andrew telling Quinn how to undertake the delegated work – he simply talked in terms of expected outcomes.

Andrew concluded by saying, "With these guidelines in place I trust you to decide where action needs to be taken, and I believe that you can manage all of these situations accordingly. It's your responsibility now."

With those closing words Quinn was conscious of feeling an unparalleled surge of excitement and empowerment. Andrew rose from his chair, thereby making a clear statement that the meeting was over. Andrew smiled at Quinn, said thank you, and moved off towards his desk taking his tablet with him. Quinn left the office thanking Elizabeth on the way out. On the way back down to the second floor Quinn reflected on the strange reality of now working, for the first time, for a VP who was able to conduct efficient meetings in 15 minutes, was extremely businesslike, yet still seem somehow friendly and approachable. This was going to take some getting used to!

Quinn sat down in the office again and surveyed the chaos that had been created in the first five days. So, thought Quinn, I have just had added a significant workload to my already busy existence from all of those items that Andrew has just delegated to me. How on earth am I going to cope, sighed Quinn?

3. SYMPTONS OF POOR DELEGATION

Quinn spent the remainder of that morning in what was now rapidly becoming a familiar pattern - endless telephone calls and email alerts constantly interrupting any attempt Quinn made at concentration on more important issues. The various boxes containing Quinn's personal effects from previous jobs and home still sat unpacked around the office space.

Lunchtime eventually arrived and Quinn decided to take a long walk. Stratum's office building was situated at the most northerly end of the business park and was adjacent to one of the city's parks – a popular place for lunchtime walks and runs amongst the Stratum staff.

Quinn was finding it difficult to forget the image and sensation of the calm, order and serenity of Andrew the VP. The ease with which he had delegated a vast array of tasks that morning had made Quinn feel completely, and comfortably, responsible and accountable for them. Andrew had however also made it clear that he would ultimately be accountable for the end result, but that he trusted Quinn to deliver. Quinn thought about the chaos waiting n the office and a variety of tasks that, even after just one week, were beginning to become overwhelming.

Symptoms of Poor Delegation

Quinn had reached the entrance to the park and began a gentle walk along the central path. How could I ever to get to that state of efficiency, thought Quinn? Am I perhaps a product of my previous environments? In particular Quinn thought back to that last job and the organization looking for clues from the experience. After some ten minutes of quiet reflection Quinn could begin to see where the delegation habits, or more importantly the lack of delegation, practiced by the leaders and managers in that organization had a significant impact. Comparing the experiences with Andrew this morning, and the culture he was promoting, enabled Quinn to identify a number of symptoms from that last organization:

1. Deadlines across the organization were frequently missed; in fact Quinn could really only recall one occasion when a deadline was actually met!

2. Across the organization employees, some of them friends of Quinn, often appeared to be much busier than many others. Quinn knew from personal experience what it meant to be far busier than many others.

3. Quinn had often been frustrated and occasionally bored - a trait Quinn knew was shared by many others.

4. Many of the organization's managers

were often too busy to talk to their employees.

5. There was confusion right across the organization as to where authority and responsibility correctly sat. How different to this morning's session with Andrew and the clear boundaries that had been established.

6. Quinn's ideas, and the ideas of the other employees, were frequently overlooked by managers, or even worse ignored completely.

7. Quinn recalled operating objectives constantly changing, with those changes rarely being passed down in any detail to employees charged with undertaking the delegated work.

8. Communication within the organization had been painfully slow, and in some cases even non-existent, particularly between managers and their employees.

9. Meetings seem to drag on for hours without any sense of an outcome. Again how different to that efficient fifteen minutes with Andrew this morning.

10. Quinn had been conscious that

decision making right across the organization had been very slow, inconsistent in delivery, and in some cases even non-existent. In fact the lack of decision-making was often paralyzing the ability of the organization to function properly.

11. Quinn's work, and that of many colleagues, had been frequently interrupted by the micromanaging of their workloads by their managers, and occasionally even higher-level management. Even when decision-making powers had been delegated, the reality was that managers still insisted on all decisions, and all information, being passed through them. Again paralysis struck across the organization on a frequent basis.

12. This micromanagement also led to a complete lack of trust across the organization.

13. Quinn's own manager was often seen leaving the office late at night, often taking bags of work home, especially at weekends. On several occasions Quinn's manager postponed or even cancelled entire vacations because of the critical workload.

Yes, for Quinn, that previous organization had been barely functioning. It was one of the primary reasons Quinn began looking for alternative employment. Now, less than six days into that new job, Quinn was feeling a sense of déjà vu in that it was the previous organization's practices manifesting itself in Quinn's immediate office and behaviour.

During the chaos of the first week Quinn had met only briefly with the four direct reports in her division and, as Quinn exited the park and walked back towards Stratum's building, Quinn made the decision to investigate how those four were handling their workloads. In addition how did they perceive delegation was being managed amongst the division?

Quinn walked back into the office. At the very least, thought Quinn, I have made the immediate decision that the only way to survive (and then having survived to be able to function at a highly productive and efficient level),

I must learn to delegate effectively, and practice it on a daily basis.

4. THE FEAR OF DELEGATION

Quinn had four directly reporting managers – Mark (who managed the sales team), Lucy (head of divisional marketing), Maria (who managed the delivery of face-to-face training solutions) and Ian (who managed the delivery of on-line training solutions). Quinn sent an email-meeting request to all four of them for a 10 AM meeting the next morning.

Quinn Meets the Four Managers

They all assembled the next morning as requested in one of the third floor conference rooms. The room was rectangle in shape, with three walls containing very large white boards, the fourth wall being a window. A ceiling mounted LCD projector faced the opposite wall to the window. A large drop down screen was mounted in a ceiling recess. Quinn had moved the modular furniture into a U shape, with the open end of the shape facing the end wall.

After the usual round of pleasantries and social and professional updates (Quinn was surprised to glance at the clock and see that this usual interaction had already eaten up 10 minutes of the meeting time) Quinn outlined the levels of delegation that had been passed down from Andrew yesterday.

Quinn informed the group that whilst welcoming such freedom and clarity, particularly around accountability and responsibility, this additional set of tasks would clearly have an impact on the workload that Quinn was already expected to complete. Quinn was therefore thinking about how delegation currently works (or doesn't work) in the division because there was going to have to be some form of realignment of work levels to ensure that all the division's tasks were still completed.

"The aim of this meeting therefore," began Quinn, "is for each of you to describe to me your approach and your thoughts on delegation within the Stratum Group. In particular I want to hear about how things are done within this division, both the good and the bad. I will then take that information away, process it, and look to meet with you again fairly soon to see if we can find a way of improving our operation."

Quinn picked up a blue marker pen, moved to the large central white board to capture themes and ideas. Quinn looked at the four and said to Mark, "Perhaps you could start Mark with your thoughts."

"Well I don't think it's any surprise to most people here that I'm not a great fan of delegation. I often find it's quicker and easier frankly to do things myself. I know I can do the work better than anybody else in my team." Mark, as the head of sales, was undoubtedly the most self-confident individual in the room thought Quinn.

Such a bold beginning served to almost paralyze the meeting into inactivity! Quinn, spotting the hesitancy, quickly turned to Lucy and asked her for her thoughts.

"I always think that my staff are going to push back against any attempt that I make to give them additional responsibilities. I have a small team, six including myself, and we work very closely together. Although I'm here to manage and lead them I really don't want to be disliked by them. Therefore any action that I take that is going to see them turn potentially hostile towards me frankly worries me. I know that sounds a little soft but it's worked up 'til now."

"You really think the staff will resent you if you give them additional work?" asked Quinn. "Yes I do," replied Lucy. "Everybody is already overworked and I can't load anything else onto them."

"Perhaps I'm the odd one out in the room," said Maria, "but I really don't know how I could get through the day without delegating. Although I could clearly undertake many of the tasks that I delegate, often even in my sleep, and often I have to acknowledge that it would be more fun to do them myself, the question I always ask myself is this really the most effective use of my time?"

Maria continued, "In the past I'd always found that the most common reason that I didn't delegate was because it would take a lot of initial upfront effort on my part to do it properly, and I never really had the time to invest in it. It then becomes a vicious circle when I came to realize that I would never free up time to do my important work if I didn't delegate, but I had to free up time to be able to delegate properly!"

Quinn was taking lots of quick notes as the conversation moved more confidently around the room. Quinn then looked at Ian, the fourth member of the group, and the most reserved, for an input.

"For me it's more a question of losing control," said Ian.

"I agree!" interjected Mark a little too loudly.

"No surprise there." said Lucy sarcastically. "Let's just stay focused here please." said Quinn sharply looking around the room at all four people.

Ian continued, "In my more technical side of the operation I always feel, and perhaps wrongly, that the people I am delegating to would actually do a better job than me, which would undermine my position. Moreover, if I don't have complete control then I become dispensable and my position becomes insecure."

Quinn finished making a note on the board, put down the pen, and said to the group, "There is an underlying feeling here that people are perhaps in fear of losing their jobs or their positions. Am I right?"

"Well," said Mark, "that was certainly the position a couple of years ago but I guess in all fairness since Andrew our VP arrived 12 months ago the situation has improved dramatically and I certainly don't feel the fear that used to be here before."

The others in the room nodded in agreement, even Ian.

Concerns Over Delegation

The conversation then continued around the room with some agreement and some disagreement on how delegation happens within Stratum and their division. Quinn continued to take notes. Looking across the board, as the conversation came to a close, Quinn noted the following growing list of issues and concerns:

1. Loss of power.
2. Loss of authority.
3. Loss of job satisfaction.
4. Lack of confidence in the employees to do the job satisfactory.
5. It takes too long to explain the details of every task.
6. Lack of experience and capabilities in the employees to undertake the task to the same standard that the leaders would be able to do it.

7. Consistently hearing of a lack of time to be able to delegate properly.

It was now one hour since they had started the meeting and Quinn felt the discussion had gone far enough, and was in danger of recycling the same old information. Calling the meeting to a close Quinn thanked everyone for their input and said they would get together again in the next couple days with some thoughts and ideas.

Well, thought Quinn once back in the office, I seem to have three managers (Lucy, Maria, Ian) who are either capable of delegating or are actually delegating at the moment. Mark appears a bit more of a problem, but maybe he is one of those individuals that just needs to have a system put in place for him that he can then follow.

Clearly there is some scope here for me to be able to delegate, considered Quinn, but how do I overcome these common themes of lack of confidence in the employees to do the job, lack of time to do it properly, and this sense that people will be losing control and power by delegating?

Quinn acknowledged many of these concerns were also ones Quinn shared personally, especially the lack of time and the loss of control. Why is it all human beings have a trait of a control freak about them?

5. "WHAT IS IT THAT I CAN'T DELEGATE?"

It was 2 days later and Quinn was sitting at the small conference table in the VP Andrew's office. Quinn had requested a meeting with Andrew to seek his advice and guidance on the subject of delegation and what had been revealed in the meeting with the direct reports. Andrew had been enthusiastic at the suggestion of exploring further the subject of delegation.

Quinn's Second Meeting With Andrew

He began the meeting by explaining that one

of his objectives was to find the right balance between having common and consistent systems and processes operating throughout his division, whilst still allowing the managers and staff the opportunity to operate with individual creativity.

In requesting the meeting Quinn had received a reply from Andrew's executive assistant Elizabeth asking that Quinn produce an agenda that would highlight the areas that needed to be covered. Item one called for Quinn to outline the current situation.

"Please do not think," began Quinn, "that I am in any way stating that I cannot cope with the responsibilities that this job presents. I think my position has enormous potential, but I would be lying if I didn't say at the moment I am a little overwhelmed at the amount that has to be done. I have been giving a lot of thought to how to better improve my time management for this role and that led me to look at one of the greatest time-saving tools - delegation."

Andrew sat passively with his tablet

computer in front of him, gently making notes with his fingertip on the screen. "I'm glad that we're having this discussion now and not four months down the line, which is when most people in my experience suddenly realize they are unable to see the wood from the trees." smiled Andrew.

Quinn explained about the meeting with the four managers and how collectively they were keen on delegation as a concept, but there were some barriers to overcome in terms of a perceived loss of control and, importantly, finding the time to do it properly. Quinn also stated it was clear from the meeting the managers need to have the skills and processes in place for the concept of delegation to be effective. If this could happen Quinn believed they would be able to delegate more of their tasks down to the appropriate level.

"That's one of the keys to this whole subject of delegation," said Andrew, "in finding the ultimate level of capability in an organization where the tasks should sit. Just because responsibility for a task, or even accountability, is in your job description that doesn't necessarily mean that's where the physical undertaking of the task necessarily has to sit."

Item two on the agenda was an opportunity for Andrew to present his thoughts on how he saw delegation operating within his division.

Andrew's Thoughts on Delegation

Andrew began "Delegation itself is simple. Organizations and people that do the simple things well become hugely effective. However, in my view, in reality nothing is more fraught with difficulties than the subject of delegation. The difficulties and challenges of doing everything yourself usually leads to stress, burnout and very often missing crucial deadlines."

Andrew looked at Quinn, "There's nothing wrong acknowledging that you do not have all the requisite skills to undertake your job, I'm pleased to see that you already think you might be stretched too thin and perhaps at capacity. Both of these should be taken as strong indicators that it's time to delegate. I'm pleased you reached that point so early on."

Andrew continued, "I need you to think in terms of your overall effectiveness and I need you to focus on where it's best to allocate your time and your talents. Being an effective leader is making sure that you allocate your talents where they can make the biggest difference and the biggest impact. As you've already said if you can delegate tasks to others, help free up your time, this can multiply your overall effectiveness as a leader and the contribution you make to this organization".

"Looking at your managers I like to think in terms of benefits of delegating. It will teach them how to communicate persuasively, how to train others, how to coach, how to supervise and, above all, how to help them build and maintain highly effective teams".

"Powerful delegation pushes the decision-making authority down through the structure of our organization. Our challenge as leaders is to find the appropriate level where that decision-making should ultimately rest. You have to find the right person to undertake that work. I don't want to oversimplify this but if I was to ask you to leave here today with one sentence in mind to move forward I would say to you:

You need to choose the right tasks today to delegate, identify the right people to delegate those tasks to, and then delegate the task in the correct and consistent manner."

Quinn was nodding in agreement, as well as making notes. Much of what Andrew said resonated with Quinn, and it was clear from the limited interactions with him so far that he didn't just talk about the subject, but it underpinned his working ethics and ethos.

"Thanks," said Quinn, "I know in persuading others to undertake things we should always try and talk in terms of benefits, so I put Item three on the agenda as an opportunity for me to find out from you what you see as the major benefits of being able to delegate effectively. With some of my team clearly already feeling they are overworked, and without the capacity to take on extra tasks, I need to be persuasively armed to convince the team that buying into effective delegation can help everybody."

"I couldn't agree more." said Andrew. Items three on the agenda was headed 'Benefits'.

Andrew paused, collecting his thoughts, and gazed briefly out of the window.

Benefits to the Organization

He began, "If we start at the organizational level, I think the most important benefit is of strategic importance. The organization needs the correct kind of culture within it. That culture is one of trust. The gift of trust will generate an answering trust. That becomes the foundation of building a highly effective organization. Delegation is also, from an organizational perspective, an important way in which to cascade down the vision and objectives of an organization - down to the grassroots."

Benefits to Employees

"If we think about our employees here is my shortlist of the key benefits." Andrew opened the buff coloured file in front of him and extracted a single plain piece of paper and handed it across to Quinn. Quinn looked at the paper, which had a header on it of 'Benefits to the Employee'. Beneath it were listed the following:

1. The provision of professional growth opportunities.

2. The enhancement of self-confidence and the value that the individual adds to the organization.

3. Personal satisfaction and a strong sense of achievement.

4. Opportunities for employees to be involved in decision-making.

5. The development of increased professional knowledge and new skills.

6. An improved sense of, and understanding of where, the organization is

heading, through greater involvement in the process.

"Any questions on the list?" asked Andrew.

Quinn read through the list 3 times to make sure it made sense and replied, "No thank you. It makes perfect sense."

Benefits to Leaders

"In which case let me give you my thoughts on benefits to the managers and leaders." said Andrew as he extracted the second sheet of paper from the file and slid it across the table to Quinn.

This single sheet contained the header 'Benefits to the Leader' and Quinn looked down the following list:

1. It will make your job easier and exciting.

2. It reduces stress.

3. It will enhance your reputation.

4. It develops trust and rapport with all of your staff.

5. It frees up valuable time to enable you

to do more effective work.

"Any questions on that list?"

Quinn smiled and said no.

Definitions

Quinn looked down at the agenda on the table and Item four headed 'Definitions'.

"I know from what I've seen so far," said Quinn "you're very comfortable with your experience in delegating, and I believe you probably have a system that you use to help you be consistent." Quinn looked for affirmation from Andrew. He nodded in agreement.

Quinn continued, "So I thought it would be helpful if you could give me some definitions of the keywords, from your perspective, that I can then cascade down my division to help that continuation and consistency take place".

"The 3 words I had in mind," continued Quinn, were 'authority', 'accountability', and 'responsibility'."

Andrew extracted the third piece of

paper from the file in front of him and handed it to Quinn. Quinn was beginning to marvel at the way in which Andrew had prepared for this meeting. They were already on item four and the meeting had barely lasted 15 minutes. This was in no small part to the precision and clarity that Andrew was able to bring through his prior preparation.

Quinn looked at this particular document, which was headed up 'Definitions'. The three words were listed with a sentence beside each of Andrew's definitions:

Authority. This is the appropriate amount of power given to an individual or a group by delegation, which includes the right to act to make decisions.

Accountability. This defines that the person being delegated to must answer for his or her or their actions and decisions.

Responsibility. This is the task itself and the intended results, and the ability to set clear expectations of outcomes.

Quinn read the three definitions and thanked Andrew for the clarity.

Five Steps to Delegation

Item five on the agenda was headed 'How to Delegate'.

"I was a little surprised to see this item on the agenda", said Andrew.

"I put it on there," replied Quinn "because I wanted to ensure that any delegation system that I setup was consistent with the one that you use." Quinn felt somewhat defensive.

"What I'm going to do," replied Andrew, "is give you five areas to focus on - areas I use on a consistent basis, and I want you to develop them as you see fit. As long as you stay within these five areas you and I will be singing from the same sheet."

"Those five areas, and I suggest you always delegate in this order, are:

1. The desired results, and I don't mean *how* to do the task, but rather what it should look like at the end, the outcome.

2. The guidelines that will apply.

3. The resources available.

4. The boundaries of accountability.

5. The consequences, the good and bad!"

"You've got very capable staff working for you, and I believe that within those five areas you can develop a robust enough system that can be consistently applied. Any questions?"

Quinn could not have hoped for a more clear and concise answer, and said so.

Delegation Boundaries

Item six on the agenda was headed 'Boundaries'. "In Item five," began Quinn, "I wanted to see if there were any issues, from your perspective, that should not be delegated, or perhaps where caution should be exercised."

"There aren't many no-go areas from my view," replied Andrew, "but a couple of more common sense issues I think are worthy of mentioning."

"Key HR issues would be the first I would suggest. Any issues such as hiring, firing or any form of disciplinary action I would be very reluctant to delegate. I would add to that morale issues in your teams and any problems linked to that, such as absenteeism rates, poor levels of motivation. Also anything that has been delegated to you personally, most likely by me, where the expectation was it was being personally delegated to you."

"Finally, although we're always looking to develop our employees through the delegation process, I would be cautious of delegating a task to a team when nobody in that team is qualified to undertake the work. I could quantify that by adding part of the delegation process could be to identify the appropriate remedial training required which would then enable the delegation to take place afterwards."

Quinn had made a quick list of these on the notepad. The last item on the agenda was headed 'Any questions'. Andrew asked Quinn if there was any other areas they should cover and after a moment of thought Quinn said "No thank you."

Andrew said, "I think I would just like to add on to the last item about boundaries. I would suggest you start every day not with the thought of "what should I delegate", but rather, "what is it that I cannot delegate?" I believe if you were to approach every working day with that simple statement in mind, and if all of your managers and team leaders follow that lead, we would have an incredibly powerful organization."

Andrew continued, "As a leader I look to you to undertake your most important role and that is to find the appropriate time to *think*, to *plan* and to *control*. In other words I need you to be strategic. Force yourself to focus on the important."

"I cannot thank you enough." said Quinn smiling. "There's enough here for me to go back to my managers and begin to set some boundaries and put in place systems and processes. I really want them to be part of the solution."

"And I," replied Andrew, "would like to know how you get on."

"Please come and see me before the end of next week and let me know what the outcome is."

On that note Andrew stood up, his standard way of letting you know that the meeting was concluded, thanked Quinn for the agenda and for tackling what Andrew believed to be one of the most important strategic tasks in the organization. He turned his back and returned to his desk. Quinn left Andrew's office armed with many exciting new ideas.

6. CREATING AMAZING DELEGATION

The final delegation meeting took place the following Monday. Quinn had called the four managers back to the third floor conference room and had let them know they would be using the meeting to build a delegation model they could all use - therefore creating a consistent system within the division.

The Final Meeting

Quinn was once again positioned by the large whiteboard in the conference room and appointed Lucy as the person to capture all of the notes taken from the day through a combination of handwritten notes and taking digital photographs of the whiteboards as they were filled up.

"After our meeting last week," began Quinn, "I met with Andrew to get his thoughts and feedback on the idea that we might create a common delegation model in our division. Andrew was extremely enthusiastic about the idea, and gave me a number of suggestions as to the route we should go down. What I want to do this morning is collect our thoughts around the following," Quinn turned to the whiteboard and began to write the following list:

Definitions.

What to delegate.

When to delegate.

Whom to delegate to.

Reviewing tasks delegated.

Designing a template for us all to use.

"Other any questions on these?" Quinn surveyed the room and was met by smiles and nodding in agreement.

"Good, then let's get going." Quinn picked up the marker again and turned to the white board to the left of the main board. Quinn wrote out the definitions from Andrew for 'Accountability', 'Authority', 'Responsibility'.

"These are key definitions, so I'm going to leave them here on this board all the time to help keep us focused," said Quinn.

Quinn then returned to the main board and wrote a large header 'Benefits'.

Four Benefits to Delegation

"Based on our discussion the other day, the discussions I've had with Andrew, and also looking at my previous experiences, I believe there are four key benefits to delegation." Quinn wrote on the board:

1. Free up our committed and valuable

time.

2. Use our energy on the things that matter most and those that are the most important.

3. Personal and professional development of our employees.

4. Learning who you can trust within your team and those who are around you.

"Are those in priority order?" asked Mark.

"I hadn't thought of it that way," replied Quinn, "but looking at the list I would say yes they are in priority. Time is our most valuable resource and control of it should be everybody's priority. It logically follows we can't focus on the most important issues until we have control of our time so that should be number two. As leaders one of our most important functions is coaching and mentoring, which involves the development of our staff - which is number three. Lastly, it's not until we develop them that we really learn who we can trust – number four."

"I certainly have no problem with that

list being a priority list." added Maria. Ian nodded his agreement as well.

"Good." concluded Quinn. "Let's move on."

Lucy photographed the whiteboard with her smart phone. Quinn cleared the board ready for the next stage. Quinn wrote at the top 'What to delegate'.

What to Delegate

Quinn invited a general discussion now on what the four in the room felt would be appropriate to delegate. The whiteboard quickly filled up with a range of ideas, which they gradually began to group together. Quinn then suggested grouping these many concepts into more general areas and the following four big headings emerged on the whiteboard:

1. The making of day-to-day minor decisions.

2. Minor staffing issues such as scheduling, shift changes etc.

3. Anything the employees could be

expected to do when you the leader were not there.

4. Any tasks that could develop employees in other areas for potential promotion and skills development.

"I'm beginning to think it's very important to let our employees think more for themselves," said Mark, "such as answering routine questions or enquiries. I think the only way I can get over my control issues is if I know that the guys are developing the necessary creative skills to be able to cope without constant supervision from me." Quinn smiled, encouraged that progress was being made, especially if the more skeptical member of the group was beginning to see some benefits.

"The best way to start the day is to ask the question", Quinn told the group what Andrew had said, "what can I not delegate". "I'm beginning to see now why he's such an effective vice president." said Lucy somewhat sarcastically. "Well it's certainly working," added Maria, "so whatever he's doing I think it's hugely important that we all follow suit". The others laughed.

When to Delegate

"So that's the *what*," said Quinn, "now we move on to the *when*". Again Lucy took some photographs of the whiteboard before Quinn cleaned it off started to write again.

Ian felt that the best way they should approach the 'when' issue was to develop a form of questions they should be asking themselves as part of the delegation process. "Isn't this all a little bit systematized?" interjected Mark.

"I think Ian is on the right track," added Maria, "and I think as with all concepts like this after awhile these questions will become second nature to us all and won't require us to slavishly follow a system - because it will become just another good habit".

Quinn looked around the group for a general consensus and everybody was nodding. After some fifteen minutes of debate five key areas emerged that could form the basis of the questions they would need to ask themselves. Quinn grouped them on the board as follows:

1. Do I have enough time to delegate this task effectively? For example is training required; do I have the time to monitor the progress; is there time to rework the project if it goes off target? etc.

2. Is this a task that I personally should delegate? This cross refers back to the 'what to delegate', essentially to make sure there is a final check in place that items which are genuinely strategically important need our personal attention are not delegated.

3. Is this a task that someone else can do? Is there someone on the team who already has, or can be given, the appropriate expertise and data to complete the task?

4. Does the delegation of this task provide opportunities to develop and grow employees' skills?

5. Is this a task that will reappear or become repetitive, in the same or similar form, in the future?

Who to Delegate to

"Well this leads us neatly into deciding to whom we should delegate, as that subject is re-occurring more and more frequently in our dialogue here this morning." announced Quinn.

"As I think I've said many times," added Mark, "this is an area where, getting it right, will be the difference between us sinking or swimming."

"I don't wish to sound egotistical but I'm head of my department because I'm a damn good salesman," he added. "In fact, a better salesman than anybody in my team. In my mind anything I delegate is going to come back at a lesser standard then I would have achieved myself. That's why I have such a problem with delegation."

Quinn turned to Maria, who Quinn believed was more comfortable than anybody else in the group at the moment with delegation and asked for her opinion. "In delegating work to others," began Maria, "we have to accept that they may not do it as well as us, in fact they may do it differently, but that does not mean that they do not produce work that is acceptable. It's that phrase "good enough" that we should frequently ask ourselves. "Is it good enough?" And I think you'll find on the majority of occasions that the answer is yes it is."

Quinn addressed Mark, "I think that no matter what we decide this morning Mark this area is going to be difficult for you. I know it can be very challenging for me as well. But we owe it to ourselves, and this urgent need to get a better control of our time to become more effective as individuals, to give it a try."

Mark looked at the other three members of the group for reassurance and found them all sitting comfortably, gently nodding in agreement. "Okay," he said, "frankly at this stage I am willing to try anything to reduce my workload to a more manageable and effective level."

Lucy had finished photographing the board again and Quinn wrote the new heading

'To whom' at the top. It was necessary for Quinn to take over at this stage, as it was clear the group was struggling with this area to achieve any clarity of thinking on the subject.

"I think we should consider three factors here." suggested Quinn. On the board Quinn mapped out the following three areas:

1. What is the current workload of the person or group that we're thinking of delegating too? For example do they have the time to take on more work? If you do delegate to this person or group is there going to have to be some rescheduling of current workloads and responsibilities? Some form of re-prioritization?

2. Looking at the delegated task, and the skills and experience required, how closely aligned are those to the person or group that we are planning to delegate to?

3. How well do we know the person or group to whom we are delegating? Is this individual or group very independent; are their interests and goals aligned with the task we are thinking of delegating? Is there an

opportunity through this delegation to bring them more closely aligned with a bigger organizational goal or objective?

Quinn added, "I think the key to this area is we have got to know the values of our employees, we have to get to know them as people. I doubt if we truly know how motivated they are, what experience they have in their past jobs and tasks. We may even think they are busy because that's our perception of how they look, whereas in fact been maybe just adopting Parkinson's Law, "work expands to fill the time available for its completion". We need to find the time to ask them about themselves and most importantly we need to listen to the answers."

"Whichever way we turn we seem to come back to finding that all elusive time", said Lucy.

"Which leads us into our final area," continued Quinn, "that of the review process."

The Review Process

Quinn turned again to Maria and asked if she had any thoughts on this area, as she appeared to be delegating a degree of her work already. Maria thought for a while and then said, "I think the review process is essential, as this really is the opportunity where we can establish standards and maintain control, which I know is important to several in the room (she looked directly at Mark!). I know we can talk about time again, and we have already said that time is our biggest issue, but there is no point in delegating a task if we do not factor in throughout its process that we owe it to the person we are delegating to to be available to check on progress."

"Well I also think," added Ian, "that without a review process how will we ever know if the task is on schedule? How do we stop it heading towards failure? I would think nobody would be willing to accept a delegated task from us without us saying we will be checking with you on a regular basis. That's really our vote of confidence to that individual to say we're here for you."

Quinn was delighted with the way this meeting was now progressing. There was uniformity of thinking around the room, and even the skeptic Mark had begun to become fully engaged in the process.

"I don't think there's any need to really record much of this discussion," said Quinn, "other than to ensure that we factor in a review process into our template model. Are we all agreed with that?" The group nodded in assent.

"So, now let's conclude this part of the meeting by just talking about what is going to happen if delegation fails." stated Quinn. "Now we're getting down to the meat of the real issue." interjected Mark. "I like to live by the Apollo 13 maxim of "failure is not an option" in my team," he said with a perhaps an unnecessary air of arrogance. However, observed Quinn, nobody in the team appeared to be in awe of him, in fact Lucy and Maria were trying to stifle giggles!

Trying to ignore that interjection from

Mark, Quinn continued, "What I'm trying to get across here is what if the task actually fails; what if the delegation that we put in place was not good enough and the people that we gave it to just didn't complete the task effectively? What happens next?"

Quinn looked around the room for answers. When no one initially offered an opinion it was eventually Maria who spoke up. "My view would be you couldn't apportion blame to anyone. I would have delegated it, it was a decision that I made, so ultimately the responsibility for the failure to achieve, and the poor performance, has to remain with me individually."

"Absolutely," said Quinn, "that's exactly the line we need to take. We're paid to make decisions at the appropriate level, but we have to take responsibility for our actions. There's a whole range of things that we would then most likely go through in reviewing how it happened through analysis. We can learn from our lessons and move forward.

However, the key point to finish this

element of the meeting is that delegation carries with it an element of risk, and we just need to make sure we manage that risk appropriately. Again as leaders risk management is a key part of the skills we're expected to have."

7. THE DELEGATION TEMPLATE

After a short break to get some coffee the team reassembled in the conference room. Quinn shared with the group on the whiteboard the five key principles that Andrew had explained to use with any template model:

1. The desired results.

2. The guidelines that will apply.

3. The resources available.

4. The boundaries of accountability.

5. The consequences, the good and bad!"

"Our task now," began Quinn, "is to put some meat behind each of these five principles so we develop a template that we can start to use immediately. This template must become a habit and we must apply it consistently across our division for it to be successful. Finally, you will see that this very much follows Andrew's style - if we delegate using this template we will have clear, upfront, mutual understanding and commitment regarding the delegation."

The Delegation Model

Quinn wrote the first heading on the board as 'Desired results to be achieved'. The group then discussed, and eventually agreed on, the following definition:

Desired Results

1. We should always strive to delegate to the lowest possible organizational level. The employees who are closest to the work are often best suited for the task, because they

often have the most intimate knowledge of the detail of the day-to-day work. In addition we are looking for ways to increase our workplace efficiency.

Having determined the correct person or group qualified to undertake the delegation, explain the desired result or outcome of the task being delegated. It is important that we talk about the result or the outcome not how to undertake the task. We need to create a clear, mutual understanding of what needs to be accomplished, focusing on what, not how, results not methods. This element of the template will require an investment of our time. We must ensure that the individual or the group understands the end result, how it will look, and by what date.

Guidelines

Quinn proceeded to write the second heading on the board as 'Guidelines for the completion of the task'. Again, after some discussion and debate the following definition was agreed:

2. We must set out guidelines that will apply to the delegation - the rules. Examples would be financial authority levels, when to ask for help and guidance, etc. We must identify the parameters and the boundaries within which the individual or group can operate. We should aim to have as few of these as possible to encourage creativity and development of growth, but a firm boundary line will need to be established.

Resources

The third heading that Quinn wrote on the board was 'Resources for the task'. The following definition emerged:

3. We must detail the resources that are going to be made available to complete the task; for example people, funding, training, equipment, etc. This also includes any time that we need to allocate to help with training.

Accountability

Quinn wrote down the fourth heading as one word 'Accountability'. There was much debate around this issue, particularly around control. The following definition was eventually agreed:

4. We must clearly explain how the accountability will work. We must detail how the individual or the group will be responsible for the outcome, but how they get to the end result is their decision. We must set up the standards of performance that are going to apply and those that would be used in the evaluation of the results. Finally, the specific timelines to apply when reporting and when the evaluation will ultimately take place.

Consequences

The final heading that Quinn wrote on the board was 'Consequences'.

This definition was the least challenging for the group to reach consensus on as follows:

5. The consequences for the task need to be laid down. For example what will happen if the task is completed as required? What happens if the task is exceeded? What are the consequences for the task not being met? Any rewards, or punishments, that will apply to this particular delegation need to be outlined.

The group also felt that soliciting questions, and regular checks of understanding, from those being delegated to throughout the process would be essential. Apart from increasing their confidence in the individual or group being delegated to, it also facilitates buy-in to the process by those individuals. The whole process must be designed to be undertaken in a collaborative, empowering atmosphere, wherever possible striving for mutual agreement.

Quinn noticed a marked change in the atmosphere and attitude of the 4 direct reports as this meeting came to a conclusion. It was clear that by reaching a common consensus there was a strong desire to make this delegation model work, and a sense that a new chapter was about to open in divisional efficiency.

"Our time is up," concluded Quinn. "Any last questions before we leave here and put this plan into place?" Quinn looked around at each person in the room individually. There were no questions, but Quinn could tell from the body language and expressions that consensus had been reached.

"Lucy, I would like you to get this template typed up and circulated to all of us for a final review tomorrow and then we can agree to move forward. We can do this by email."

"Absolutely." enthused Lucy.

"Okay then," said Quinn in an excited tone, "this has been a great session guys and I think we are on to the start of something fabulous. I want to leave you with another Andrew quote that he left me with the other day when he delegated a bunch of tasks to me. I want you to remember this and use it with your own people as much as you can, because it really lifted me, inspired me and certainly motivated me when I heard it."

"Decide where action needs to be taken and you can manage the situation accordingly. It's your responsibility now!."

The End

8. KEY LEARNING POINTS

Chapter Two

Symptoms of Poor Delegation:

1. Deadlines across the organization are frequently missed.

2. Across an organization some employees often appear to be much busier than many others.

3. Employees appear frustrated and occasionally bored.

4. Many of the organization's managers are often too busy to talk to their employees.

5. There is confusion across the organization as to where authority and responsibility correctly sit.

6. Ideas of the employees are frequently overlooked by managers, or even ignored completely.

7. Operating objectives are constantly changing, with those changes rarely being passed down in any detail to employees charged with undertaking the delegated work.

8. Communication within the organization is painfully slow and in some cases even non-existent, particularly between managers and their employees.

9. Meetings seem to drag on for hours without any sense of an outcome.

10. Decision making across the organization is very slow, inconsistent in delivery, and in some cases even non-existent. The lack of decision-making is often paralyzing the ability of the organization to function properly.

11. Employee's work is frequently interrupted by the micromanaging of those workloads by their managers, and occasionally even higher-level management.

12. This micromanagement leads to a complete lack of trust across the organization.

13. Managers are often seen leaving the office late at night, often taking bags of work home, especially at weekends. Managers postpone or even cancel entire vacations because of the critical work-load.

Chapter Three

Reasons why leaders fear to delegate:

1. Loss of power.

2. Loss of authority.

3. Loss of job satisfaction.

4. Lack of confidence in the employees to do the job satisfactory.

5. It takes too long to explain the details of every task.

6. Lack of experience and capabilities in the employees to undertake the task to the same standard that the leaders would be able to do it.

7. Consistently hearing of a lack of time to be able to delegate properly.

Chapter Four

Benefits to employees of leaders delegating effectively:

1. The provision of professional growth opportunities.

2. The enhancement of self-confidence and the value that the individual adds to the organization.

3. Personal satisfaction and a strong sense of achievement.

4. Opportunities for employees to be involved in decision-making.

5. The development of increased professional knowledge and new skills.

6. An improved sense of, and understanding of where, the organization is heading, through greater involvement in the process.

Benefits to leaders of delegating effectively:

1. It will make the leader's job easier and exciting.

2. It reduces stress.

3. It will enhance the leader's reputation.

4. It develops trust and rapport with the employees.

5. It frees up valuable time to enable leaders to do more effective work.

Definitions:

Authority. This is the appropriate amount of power given to an individual or a group by delegation, which includes the right to act to make decisions.

Accountability. This defines that the person being delegated to must answer for his or her or their actions and decisions.

Responsibility. This is the task itself and the intended results, and the ability to set clear expectations of outcomes.

The five stages of effective delegation:

1. The desired results, not *how* to do the task, but rather what it should look like at the end, the outcome.

2. The guidelines that will apply.

3. The resources available.

4. The boundaries of accountability.

5. The consequences, the good and bad!"

Chapter Five

The four major areas to delegate:

1. The making of day-to-day minor decisions.

2. Minor staffing issues such as scheduling, shift changes etc.

3. Anything the employees could be expected to do when you the leader were not there.

4. Any tasks that could develop employees in other areas for potential promotion and skills enhancement.

Five questions to ask before delegating a task:

1. Do I have enough time to delegate this task effectively? For example is training required; do I have the time to monitor the progress; is there time to rework the project if it goes off target? etc.

2. Is this a task that I personally should delegate? This cross refers back to the 'what to delegate', essentially to make sure there is a final check in place that items which are genuinely strategically important need personal attention and should not be delegated.

3. Is this a task that someone else can do? Is there someone on the team who already has, or can be given, the appropriate expertise and data to complete the task?

4. Does the delegation of this task provide opportunities to develop and grow employees'

skills?

5. Is this a task that will reappear or become repetitive, in the same or similar form, in the future?

Chapter Six

The delegation template:

1. Always strive to delegate to the lowest possible organizational level. The employees who are closest to the work are often best suited for the task, because they often have the most intimate knowledge of the detail of the day-to-day work. In addition we are looking for ways to increase our workplace efficiency. Having determined the correct person or group qualified to undertake the delegation, explain the **desired result or outcome** of the task being delegated. It is important to talk about the result or the outcome, not how to undertake the task. Create a clear, mutual understanding of what needs to be accomplished, focusing on what, not how, results not methods. This will

require an investment of time. Ensure the individual or the group understands the end result, how it will look, and by what date.

2. Set out **guidelines** that will apply to the delegation - the rules. Examples would be financial authority levels, when to ask for help and guidance, etc. Identify the parameters and the boundaries within which the individual or group can operate. Aim to have as few of these as possible to encourage creativity and development of growth, but a firm boundary line will need to be established.

3. Detail the **resources** that are going to be made available to complete the task; for example people, funding, training, equipment, etc. This also includes any time needed to allocate to help with training.

4. Clearly explain how the **accountability** will work. Detail how the individual or the group will be responsible for the outcome, how they get to the end result is their decision. Set up the standards of performance that are going to apply and those that would be used in the

evaluation of the results. Finally, the specific timelines to apply when reporting and when the evaluation will ultimately take place.

5. The **consequences** for the task need to be laid down. For example what will happen if the task is completed as required? What happens if the task is exceeded? What are the consequences for the task not being met? Any rewards, or punishments, that will apply to this particular delegation need to be outlined.

ABOUT THE AUTHOR

Mark Hollingsworth was born and raised in the United Kingdom. After a short career in the banking and insurance sectors he was commissioned into the Royal Air Force, graduating from the Royal Air Force College Cranwell in 1987. Mark saw service in the United Kingdom, Belize, Germany and Canada, serving in a variety of leadership roles in the administration branch. He retired from the Royal Air Force in 2003 in the rank of squadron leader and now lives in Canada.

Since that time Mark has gained extensive leadership experience as a CEO, Executive Director, Vice President and Director in a variety of organizations. In 2006 he published his first book on leadership ('Leadership: The Basics') and has since undertaken numerous lecturing and speaking engagements on the subject of essential leadership skills, helping him become one of the world's thought leaders in the basic skills of leadership.

www.ingramcontent.com/pod-product-compliance
Lightning Source LLC
Chambersburg PA
CBHW071607170526
45166CB00003B/1019